Nestlé
smarties
BOOK OF
WIZARDRY

Other Smarties titles available

Smarties Chuckle Factory
Smarties Hilariously Funny Verse
Smarties How to Draw Cartoons
Smarties Joke Book
Smarties Smart Art
Smarties Smart Science
Smarties Travel Teasers

Nestlé® smarties®
BOOK OF
WIZARDRY

By
JUSTIN SCROGGIE

Illustrations by
DAVID MOSTYN

First published in the UK by Robinson Children's Books,
an imprint of Constable & Robinson Ltd, 2001

Constable & Robinson Ltd
3 The Lanchesters
162 Fulham Palace Road
London
W6 9ER

A copy of the British Library Cataloguing in Publication Data
for this title is available from the British Library

ISBN 1-84119-290-2

Printed and bound in the EC

10 9 8 7 6 5 4 3 2 1

Contents

Every Wizard's
10 Commandments

You Shall Never:

1 Be rude to a frog – he might be a Prince
2 Be polite to a witch
3 Predict Lottery numbers
4 Give an elephant hiccups
5 Read a mind without permission
6 Look silly in a pointy hat
7 Change history (in case you erase yourself)
8 Make it snow in summer
9 Turn anyone into a lavatory bowl
10 Fly faster than the speed of light

The Magic Team

Wizard Waldo

So, you want to be a Wizard? H'mmmm.

My name is Waldo and I'm a VERY senior Wizard in W.W.W., the World Web of Wizards. Different Wizards have different jobs – Dragon-slaying, Spell-checking, Talent-spotting. I teach young humans to become Wizards.

A talent-spotting Wizard sent me a report last week, and it was all about YOU!

You didn't know you had a gift for Wizardry, did you? Ordinary humans usually aren't aware of their gift, and if they are they don't know how to use it! Just now I've got an apprentice called Prentiss, who is trying my patience to the limits. But I'm a very good teacher and one day – *one day!* – Prentiss will be a very good Wizard.

Now don't get too pleased with yourself. Your report wasn't *that* good. In fact, it's going to take a lot of work to dig out your Wizardness from all the usual mortal rubbish.

But . . . if I'm going to try, you'd better know a bit more about me. I live in a cottle (a cross between a cottage and a castle), deep in the forest at the end of a little-used animal track. No, you've never seen it, because I keep it hidden beneath a vast fog bank.

It's huge like a castle, but cosy like a cottage (except for some spooky rooms I use just for magical purposes).

I am a VERY POWERFUL Wizard. I can change the Weather, travel through Time, read Minds, tell Fortunes, make things appear or disappear.

But all this magical trickery is *not* what being a Wizard is all about. Power has to be used wisely, or not at all.

If only my neighbour Witch Grewsum understood that!

3

Prentiss

My name's Prentiss, and I've been "sent" to Waldo to be trained in the art of Wizardry. I thought learning to be a Wizard was going to be wicked! Think again.

Everything's so old here. I mean, I'm a 21st-century kid. You know – sweatshirt, jeans, trainers, cable TV. This 'cottle' is like the Middle Ages, and I have to wear this stupid hat to show I'm a Learner. As if I didn't know.

Everyone thinks I'm stupid, 'cos I'm always getting things wrong – spilling potions, turning things into peculiar objects, making weird weather. It's not my fault if the spells don't work properly. I blame the teacher personally.

I've got one friend and one enemy out here in Nowheres-ville. My friend is the Witch next door, Grewsum. OK, she's not a very clever Witch, and actually I think she's just nice to me to get at Waldo. But hey – any friend's better than no friend at all, and Grewsum knows some really cool stuff. Even if she can't make any of it work!

My arch-enemy is Hairball, Waldo's excuse for a cat. Hairball is like a piranha with fur – sort of fluffy, gothic punk. He used to be a vampire cat, and Waldo thinks he's sweet. Hairball thinks I'm really dumb, and he teases and tricks me all the time.

Actually, I think Waldo's OK, and if I'm honest I want to impress him and be a good Wizard. Just don't tell anyone I said that!

5

Hairball

Fancy yourself as a Wizard, eh? There's one born every minute . . .

Hi, I'm Hairball, ex-vampire Cat and the coolest Cat around. I used to be really evil and sly (the story of my life with Wicked Witch Voltingross is on page 38) but now I'm a good Cat. Honest. No, really. Well, most of the time.

Waldo's my boss, and he's a seriously powerful Wizard. Trouble is, he just wastes his time with these hopeless apprentices!

Now, I'm not saying *you* are hopeless. In fact, you might just turn out to be a promising Wizard (I've seen your file). But Prentiss is truly the most stupid boy I've ever scratched. He makes plankton look brainy. Of course I tease him! Who else is going to show him what an idiot he is? I'm doing him a favour.

My only problem with Waldo is the Rat called Nat who lives in his hat. Now, I'm a Cat, OK? I think like a cat, I make catty remarks and I behave like a cat. You know: Eat, Sleep, Cover myself in Spit. To me, Nat is 'on the menu', know what I mean? Every time I look at Waldo's hat I see lunch.

Anyway, good luck with your shot at Wizardry. You can't be any worse than Prentiss!

Nat-the-Rat-in-his-Hat

Yo! Like, hi! I'm Nat (short for Natalie – but don't tell!).

I'm the girl-power round here and I have a neat little home inside Waldo's Hat. Mostly I'm on his collar, or as I call it, 'the patio'.

I'm not into this Wizard thing, you know. I mean, sure, I can talk to Waldo and he, like, understands, which is cool, but all this Spell stuff, it's so . . . macho. And if you watch Waldo really carefully, like I do, you can see that a lot of the stuff he does is just a sort of trick.

Now, I think that's cool. Like, he saves up the really powerful stuff for when he needs it, and the rest of the time he pulls a fast one. I like that.

Yeah!

The Witch Grewsum

At last, anuther viktim! I mean, Frend!

Hello, Frend. I'm Grewsum, and I eggspect you've heard oreful things about me. Oh deer, you have? Well, none of it's trew. I'm a grate Witch hooze forlen on hard times (*sob*).

Sumhow I've have lost the abillitee to SPELL.

I hav wunderful spellbooks given to me by sum of the gratest Witches in the Wurld. Every day and nite I try one of there spells out. I folow the instrukshuns to the letta, and yet they always GO RONG!

Waldo thinks I'm a failyer. He duzn't understand. Hairball duzn't either. Only Prentiss, the kid. And he's about as brite as porrij.

MAGIC WORDS

Introduction

Waldo the Wizard was tidying the books in his Library when Prentiss asked him about Spells.

Magic Words

Wizard Waldo's
Y-a-w-n-i-n-g S-p-e-l-l

TRY MY MAGIC YAWNING SPELL! READ IT ALOUD AND FIND THE HIDDEN 'YAWNS.' YAWN AS YOU SAY THEM AND YOUR FRIENDS WON'T BE ABLE TO RESIST.

Your arms are numb, your knees are bent,
Your body feels outworn.
You're nearly in the land of Nod
In bedclothes soft and warm.

With heavy eyes and lazy limbs
Your nodding head agrees
It's time you weren't awake at all
But dreaming drowsy dreams.

And deep within your noble chest
A bubble's being born,
It presses on your nose and throat
And says . . .
I want . . .
to . . .
Y-A-W-N!

11

Witch Grewsum's Itching Spell

OR TRY MY ITCHING SPELL! READ IT ALOUD IN A CREEPY-CRAWLY VOICE AND YOUR FRIENDS WILL FEEL ITCHY ALL OVER. I BET THEY START SCRATCHING.

WHAT'S WRONG WITH SCRATCHING?

ITCHING SPELL

Hubble, Bubble, Gas and Air —
Is that something in your hair?
Small and brown with sticky
  knees,
Are they lice, or eggs or fleas?

Can you feel their feathered
  fingers?
Funny how the feeling lingers!

What's that tingling? Is it ants
Crawling through your
  underpants?

Has a beetle made a nest
On your chest, in your vest?

Feel your neck hairs start to
  prickle,
Feel the bugs' antennae tickle.

In your ears, your clothes, your
  britches,
Creepy crawlies cause your itches.
However hard you try to catch
  them
It's no good, you'll have to
  scratch them!

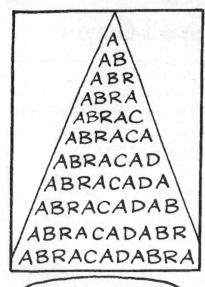

ABRACADABRA IS AN ANCIENT MAGIC WORD. IT MEANS 'GO AWAY' AND WAS OFTEN WRITTEN INSIDE A TRIANGLE.

TO ENTER THE ROBBERS' CAVE, ALI BABA JUST SAID 'OPEN SESAME' AND IT OPENED.

Waldo's Spell Cards

Waldo clicked his fingers and a pile of shimmering cards
appeared in his hand.

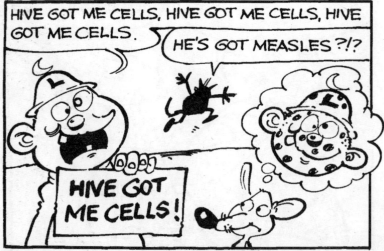

14

Witch Grewsum's
Clear-the-Room-Spell

Later, Prentiss sneaked into Witch Grewsum's foul kitchen and found this revolting recipe in her Spell Book . . .

SEARCH MY KITCHEN FOR REVOLTING ITEMS
THAT COMPLETE EACH RHYME!

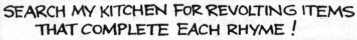

HOW TO EMPTY A ROOM IN SECONDS!

IF YOU WISH TO CAST THIS <u>SPELL</u>, FILL A POT WITH

_____

STRAIN IT THROUGH A PAIR OF <u>SHORTS</u>, ADD A CUP OF

GET SOME EARWAX—JUST A <u>LITTLE</u>, MIX IT WITH AN

_____

PUT IT IN THE POT WITH <u>CARE</u>, ADD A BALL OF

_____

TAKE THE CONTENTS OF YOUR <u>NOSE</u>, ADD A PAIR OF

_____

MAKE THIS MIXTURE YOUR PERFUME, AND YOU'LL EMPTY ANY ROOM

16

Magic Words

The Magic Door

When Waldo found out that Prentiss had been to Grewsum's house, he locked him outside. If Prentiss types in a magic word, the door will open – but what is the word?

Answer on page 121.

Nat-the-Rat's
Words of Wizzdom

An apple a day . . .

. . . Keeps the Doctor away!

Nat-the-Rat's Guide to Making a Wizard's Hat

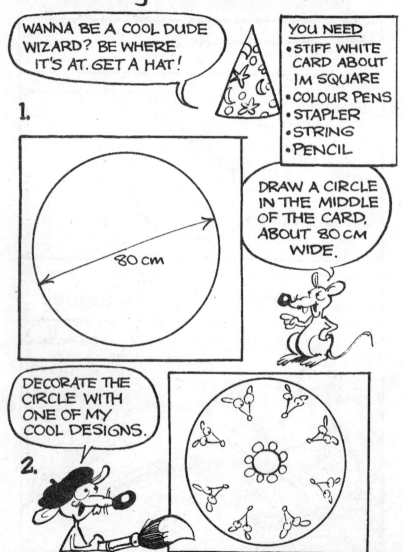

WANNA BE A COOL DUDE WIZARD? BE WHERE IT'S AT. GET A HAT!

YOU NEED
- STIFF WHITE CARD ABOUT 1M SQUARE
- COLOUR PENS
- STAPLER
- STRING
- PENCIL

1.

80 cm

DRAW A CIRCLE IN THE MIDDLE OF THE CARD, ABOUT 80 CM WIDE.

DECORATE THE CIRCLE WITH ONE OF MY COOL DESIGNS.

2.

Top Tip: Tie a long piece of string to a pencil. Hold one end of the

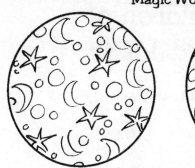

3. CUT THE CIRCLE OUT, THEN CUT STRAIGHT FROM THE EDGE TO THE CENTRE. SLIDE THE CUT EDGES OVER EACH OTHER UNTIL THE HAT FITS YOUR HEAD.

TAKE IT OFF, AND STAPLE THE EDGES TOGETHER, WITH THE METAL PRONGS OUTSIDE THE HAT.

...ring in the middle of the card, and use the pencil to draw the circle.

A Cauldron of Wizard Jokes

Why did the Wizard hit himself over the head?
So he could see stars!

Wizard 1: What has eyes but no nose, a tongue but no teeth,
and is a foot long?
Wizard 2: A Shoe!
Wizard 1: Bless you!

Why did the girl find a witch on a broomstick outside her
bedroom?
Because she left the landing light on!

Knock Knock
Who's there?
Luke
Luke who?
Luke into my crystal ball and find out!

ANIMAL MAGIC

Prentiss and the Magic Radio

For the last two hours Prentiss had been cleaning the attic of the West Tower. As Waldo said: 'Tidy wizards make tidy spells.'

Fine, thought Prentiss, except now he was covered in grime! Waldo never threw things away. The attic was full of weird junk – lamps with chocolate shades, pianos with no black notes, cut-glass waistcoats, gloomy portraits of Victorian rats, pillows stuffed with pasta. And everything was all covered in dust.

Prentiss sighed, sniffed and sneezed. A skyscraper of rubber cups quivered, swayed and collapsed in the silent way only rubber cups can. Prentiss sighed again and bent down to pick up the cups. And that's when he saw the radio.

It was very old-fashioned. The wooden case had curved corners. On the front was a large tuning dial and a dusty plastic panel. The panel glowed.

Prentiss touched the radio. It was warm under his fingers.

Odd, he thought. If the radio was on, why was there no sound? Prentiss dusted off the panel. Weird, he thought. Instead of numbers, the panel was covered with the names of animals. The dial was set on HUMAN. Strange, thought Prentiss, and without thinking he turned the dial.

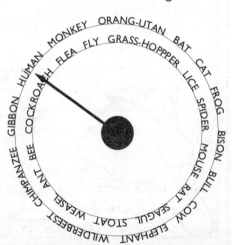

There was a loud hiss. Then a squeaky voice above his head said:

"Why are you always hanging around?"

"I'm a bat," replied another voice. "That's what we do."

"You should get around more, you know, bite some necks…"

Prentiss jumped. "Whoa! What's that?"

"Uh-oh, he's spotted us," said the first voice. "Time to fly." And with a rustle of leathery wings, two bats flew past Prentiss's nose and away. Prentiss looked at the radio. The dial was set on BAT. "It can't be," he whispered to himself. He reached out a shaking finger and turned the dial again, this time to HEAD LICE.

"Moving in?" said a tiny voice in the hair above Prentiss's left ear.

"Yeah," said another voice, "we just came from the cat. You?"

"We were all born here."

"Seems like a nice head."

"It's great. He never washes…"

"Yeeuurrrggghh!" screamed Prentiss, rubbing his hair with frantic fingers. "Get off me!"

"Weird," said the first voice calmly, "it's like he can hear us."

"I can hear you!" yelled Prentiss.

"Why is he shouting?"

"I dunno. Perhaps we should try somewhere else – his arms, legs . . ."

"Nah! I'm having a great time in this dirty head of hair."

Prentiss was about to scream again when the trapdoor of the attic crashed open and a pointy hat stuck up through the opening. An unearthly roar filled the room.

Animal Magic

"PRRRNNNNNNNTTTSSSHHH!"

Prentiss stared at Waldo. The awful sound had definitely come from him. Even now the Wizard's lips were moving, but only horrible grunty sounds were coming out.

"You what?" said Prentiss.

"SURCHUT BUCKTO HMMMMM!" roared Waldo, climbing into the attic and spinning the dial back to HUMAN.

"I said, switch it back to Human," growled Waldo.

"Sorry," said Prentiss, "Didn't understand."

"You can't understand humans when this thing is tuned to lice language. Why must you fiddle, boy?"

"Sorry," said Prentiss. "But what exactly did I fiddle with?" Waldo pointed at the radio. "It's an ASTRA – an All Species Translator. And only very senior Wizards have one."

"You don't use it much."

"I don't use it at all," snapped Waldo. "I learnt to speak Animal years ago. And until you can speak Animal, Prentiss, don't touch it."

The Wizard disappeared through the trapdoor with a bang. Prentiss turned to go, then stopped. I mustn't, he thought. But maybe, just one more go. He tiptoed back to the ASTRA and rolled the dial. It stopped at COCKROACH.

"What's all the fuss about?" said a roachy voice by his left foot.

"Just the kid."

"I thought Prentiss was asleep."

"How come?"

"I've been eating his toe nail for the last 10 minutes…"

"AAAAARRRGGGGHHH!" screamed Prentiss and ran for the trapdoor clutching his foot.

Downstairs the Wizard smiled softly.

Stripe It Lucky

Can you tell what this animal is saying?
It's all there in black-and-white!

Talking Turkey

For his first lesson, Waldo sent Prentiss into the forest with an old wand. To hear what the animals are saying, write their normal sounds in the blanks.

Animal Magic

Hairball's Guide to Cats...

How to understand what a CAT is thinking.

Happy

Friendly

Cross

Frightened

...and Dogs

How to understand what a DOG is thinking.

Happy   Friendly

Cross   Frightened

Elephant Talk

The Wizard lit a torch that made eerie shadows on the dungeon wall. To stop Prentiss getting scared, Waldo showed him how to talk to Elephants!

Witch Grewsum's Beastly Spell

When Prentiss drank Grewsum's Nettle Cider, she cast a beastly spell on him. Can you complete it by looking at Prentiss?

IF MY CIDER YOU HAVE DRUNK,
YOU WILL GROW AN ELEPHANT'S
COMB OF [   ], WINGS OF [   ]
[   ] OF VIPER, TEETH OF [   ]
TAIL OF [   ] STRIPES OF [   ]
[   ] LEGS JUST BELOW THE KNEE
THIS SPELL LASTS FOR
SEVEN DAYS!
AND IF YOU'RE BAD,
THE TAIL STAYS!

Answers on page 121.

The Worst Wizard

INVISIBILITY

Hairball and the Invisible Witch

"Why does Hairball have such large teeth?" asked Prentiss one winter's evening. It was dark outside, and the wind rattled the windows and howled down the chimney.

"All the better to eat you with," thought Hairball from beside the fire.

"Well," said Waldo, "there was once a terrible Witch called Voltingross who lived in this very forest.

"More terrible than Grewsum?" asked Prentiss.

"A thousand times more terrible," said Waldo. "Witches are usually born with a lot of Power and a bit of Mischief, or a bit of Power and a lot of Mischief. But Voltingross was born with lots of both!"

"Not good," said Prentiss.

"What she loved most was Practical Jokes," sighed Waldo. "One time she turned every bottle of shampoo into hair-remover . . .

NOT THERE!

SHAMP OOOO

". . . she once filled the public swimming pool with lime jelly, and for a whole week, dogs were taking their owners for walks!

"But," Waldo went on, "practical jokers get lonely. So Voltingross conjured up a cat as mischievous as herself."

"Hairball!" shouted Prentiss.

Waldo smiled. "At that time he was called Herrible: a cross between Terrible and Horrible. Herrible was a vampire cat: dark as a thunderstorm, with huge fangs and a taste for . . ."

"Blood?" gasped Prentiss.

"Ketchup, actually," said Waldo, "but those dripping red teeth kept many people awake at night. Then, one fateful day, the Witch learnt the secret of Invisibility! Now her naughtiness got out of hand. She pulled the Mayor's trousers down in the middle of a speech, she jumped out of people's bathtubs, just as they were getting in . . ."

"Then one day," continued Waldo, "Voltingross decided to play a sneaky trick on the most powerful Wizard in the forest – me! Her plan was hide in the chimney, make a noise like a trapped bird, wait till I looked up and then drop a bag of soot on to me!"

"Good plan," muttered Hairball.

"Bad plan," replied Waldo. "Because as soon as I got home that night I lit a fire. And that's when Voltingross realised she was stuck! She called out, of course, but all I heard was a sound like a trapped bird. And when I looked up the chimney I saw nothing."

"Why didn't she make herself visible again?"

"She couldn't reach her wand to reverse the spell because her arms were jammed. She got hotter and sweatier and smellier. And no one except Herrible knew she was there. Herrible was up on the roof, waiting for Voltingross to make her escape. She was so long he decided to jump down the chimney . . . and landed right on top of her!"

"Ouch!" said Prentiss.

"She popped out of the fireplace like a cork from a bottle, dived through the open window, and was never seen or heard of again."

"What happened to Herrible?"

"Well, you see," smiled Waldo, vampires are supposed to be bad all the time. But Herrible saved Voltingross' life. By doing a good deed, even by accident, he stopped being a vampire. I changed his fur to white, his eyes to green and his name to Hairball, and he's been with me ever since. A completely reformed character. A lovable, friendly cat."

Lovable? Friendly? Prentiss and Hairball looked at each other. For once they agreed completely:

Blind As A Bat

You can make this bat DISAPPEAR before your very eyes!!

Close your left eye. Now stare at the dot with your right eye. Hold the book at arm's length. Then move it slowly towards you until the bat disappears!

Grewsum's Vanishing Spell

Invisibility

When Prentiss tried to vanish using Grewsum's Vanishing Spell, eight objects disappeared instead! Can you draw them back in?

Answers on page 121.

How to Make an Invisibility Box

This is easy to make and will impress your friends!

YOU NEED

- A cardboard box with a lid (a shoe box is ideal)
- Black and yellow powder paints
- A Mirror
- Clear sticky tape
- Scissors
- An adult to help

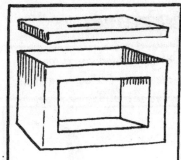

1. Make a slot in the lid large enough to put coins through. In the front panel of the box cut a window slightly smaller than the mirror.

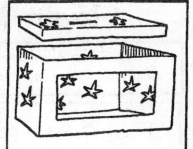

2. Paint the box and lid black inside and out and decorate all over with yellow stars.

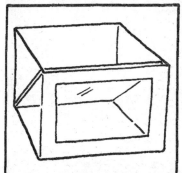

3. Lay the mirror at an angle from the base of the back panel to the top of the front panel. Secure it with sticky tape and put the lid on.

4. Drop your friends' coins, pens and keys through the slot into the box and Hey Presto – they're invisible!

Night Creature

Prentiss felt he was being watched, but in the dark forest the creature was invisible. Can you join the dots to find out what it is?

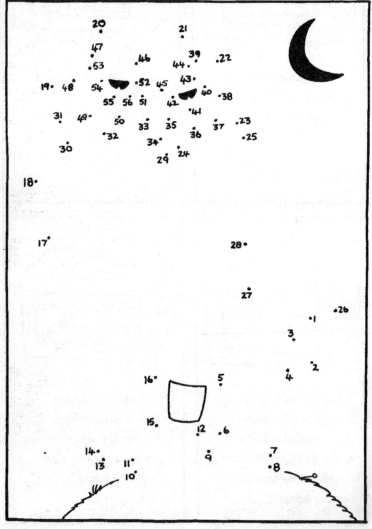

46

Answer on page 122.

The Invisible Rat

Prentiss was amazed by Waldo's 'invisible' rat, but Hairball gave the secret away . . . to you!

The Worst Wizard

FORTUNE TELLING

Palm Reading

When you're a Wizard, you can use the lines on your friends' hands to tell their future.

Here's Waldo's "handy" guide to the lines on your hands!!

WASHING LINE
Long line: Clean underwear tomorrow . . .
Short line: Stay in your room!

RAILWAY LINE
Long line: You're going on a long journey . . .
Short line: Cancelled due to driver shortage!

PHONE LINE
Long line: Get a mobile . . .
Short line: Get a life!

HEADLINE
Long line: You're in the news . . .
Short line: You're yesterday's news!

FAULT LINE
Long line: You're always up to no good . . .
Short line: But you never get caught!

CHORUS LINE
Long line: You're going to be a star . . .
Short line: Till then, you're nobody!

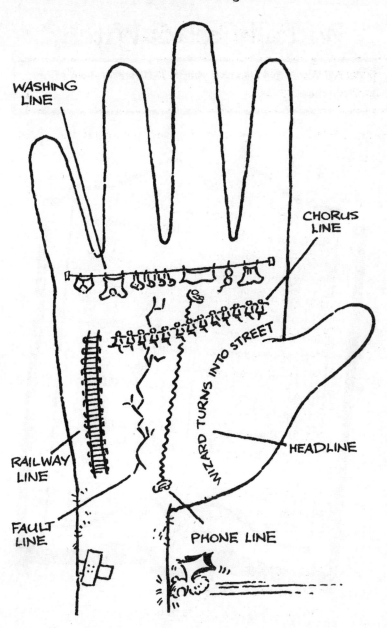

WASHING
LINE

CHORUS
LINE

WIZARD TURNS INTO STREET

RAILWAY
LINE

HEADLINE

FAULT
LINE

PHONE LINE

Fortune Telling

Witch Witch is Witch?

Wizard Waldo told Prentiss a ghastly TRUE story from his Book of Witches . . .

Over 300 years ago, there was a terrible man called Matthew the Witchfinder. His job was to track down every wicked witch in England – and destroy them!

He made up many tricks to 'prove' people were witches – all of them completely useless. One of the craziest tricks was to tie up a suspected witch and throw her in the village pond. If she floated, he said that the sacred water had rejected her, so she must really be a witch. If she sank, he said she could NOT be a witch and so she was innocent. Of course, she had usually drowned by then . . .

Witch Witch is Witch?

> *Then Waldo showed Prentiss how to do his own Witch-finding trick . . .*

Paint three eggs to look like hags with permananent ink.

Test Your Powers of Prediction

Can you predict the future? Just look at each picture panel and guess which of the three possible futures is correct.

A

1. Prentiss slips on the banana skin.
2. Prentiss steps carefully round the banana skin.
3. Hairball eats the banana skin first.

B

1. Grewsum swallows the spider and screams horribly.
2. Grewsum swallows the spider and smiles happily.
3. A Superhero saves the spider just in time.

Fortune Telling

C

1. Hairball jumps happily into the fireman's arms.
2. Hairball jumps heavily on the fireman's head.
3. The tree is hit by lightning – then Hairball jumps.

D

1. Prentiss is drenched in paint.
2. Prentiss falls down the manhole.
3. Prentiss is drenched in paint, then falls down the manhole.

SCORE 4/4 You are a prophet – well done!
3/4 You can see the future – but don't bet on it!
2/4 Probably beginner's luck
1/4 Never ever buy a lottery ticket
0/4 Seek medical help immediately.

Answers on page 122.

Crystal Ball

Prentiss has borrowed Wizard Waldo's Crystal Ball to find out what's going to happen to him tomorrow. But, being an idiot, he can't make head or tail of it. Can you?

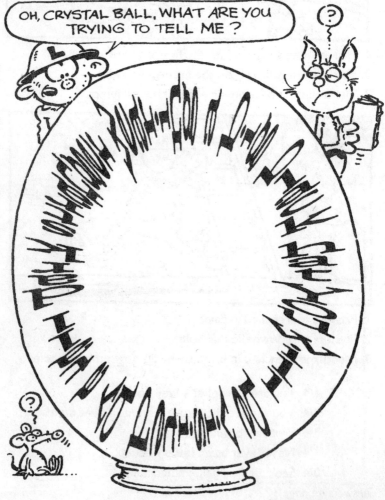

OH, CRYSTAL BALL, WHAT ARE YOU TRYING TO TELL ME?

Answer on page 122.

D.I.Y. Predictions

Predict what your friends will do tomorrow. Just ask them the questions below, fill in their answers in the Prediction Sheet on the space marked on the next page, and then read it out loud!

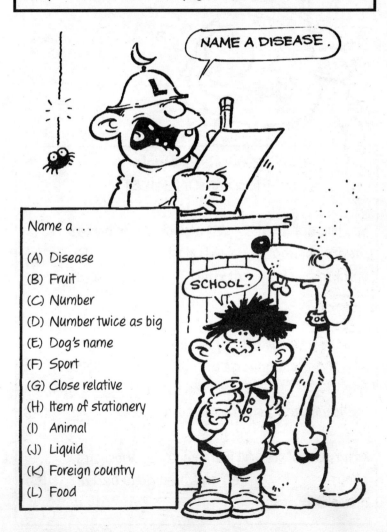

Name a . . .

(A) Disease

(B) Fruit

(C) Number

(D) Number twice as big

(E) Dog's name

(F) Sport

(G) Close relative

(H) Item of stationery

(I) Animal

(J) Liquid

(K) Foreign country

(L) Food

D.I.Y. Predictions

Grewsum's Magic
PREDICTION SHEET

You will get up at ___ (C) o'clock, after a weird
dream about a _____ (I) playing _____ (F). For
breakfast you will eat fried _____s (L) covered in
_____ (J).

At school you will study the life-cycle of the _____
(H), and the language of _____ (K). Your best
friend _____ (E) will call you a _____ (B),
but later they'll say sorry and give you _____ (A).

After school you will watch a crime show on TV
about _____ (G) and then go to bed at ___ (D)
o'clock.

Nat-the-Rat's Words of Wizzdom

A Magic Mirror of Wizard Jokes

What do you get if you cross a Wizard with an ice cube?
A cold spell!

What has a broom and
lives on the beach?
A Sandwitch!

What do you call a
Wizard spy?
James Wand!

How do Wizards drink tea?
In a cup and sorcerer!

The Wizard turned himself into a freezer.
Where did he do that?
Before my very ice!

60

HOW TO READ MINDS

Make Your Own Personality Cards

> Only Wizards are allowed their own magic Personality Cards. To make and use yours, follow Waldo's instructions below.

Cover one side of a piece of card with a Wizard pattern. Cut it into 9 squares, all the same size. On each plain side, write these words:

I hate wasps but love holidays.	I like chips but hate cabbage.	I get cross with myself sometimes.
I have a special secret.	I worry about exams.	I forget to do my homework sometimes.
I don't like being told what to do.	I'd like to be older than I am.	I lie sometimes, but I don't like liars.

How to Read Minds

1. Lay the cards in front of your volunteer, with the words face down.

2. Cast a spell over the cards.

BALLS OF CRYSTAL, ROCKS OF QUARTZ, OPEN UP YOUR DEEPEST THOUGHTS.

3. Ask your volunteer to pick any card, turn it over and read it out.

"I'D LIKE TO BE OLDER THAN I AM." THAT'S TRUE!

4. Repeat with three more cards. Take your time, and never let anyone see what the other cards say.

"I WORRY ABOUT EXAMS." I SURE DO!

Hairball's Mind Reader

Hairball decided to play a sneaky Mind Reading trick on poor Prentiss!

Think of a Number

Waldo showed Prentiss a really neat Mind Reading trick . . .

More
Mind-bending Tricks

Here are a few quick tricks to help you prove to your friends that you really are a Wizard.

DON'T LET PEOPLE TAKE TOO LONG TO THINK OF AN ANSWER.

YOUR NUMBER'S UP
Write down "37" on your palm and hide it.
Ask a friend to think of a number between 10 and 50,
in which both digits are odd.
When your friend replies: "37" (people usually do, dunno why!),
show him your mind-reading hand!

KEEP IN SHAPE
Draw a circle with a triangle inside it on your palm.
Ask a friend to quickly draw one shape inside another shape.
When your friend draws a circle with a triangle inside (people
usually do!), show her your mind-reading hand.

VEGETABLE MATTER
Draw a carrot on your palm.
Ask a friend to think of a vegetable.
When he says "carrot" (people usually do!),
show him your mind-reading hand!

How to Read Minds

Scrambled Egghead

Prentiss tried to read Waldo's mind, but some of the words were scrambled. What was Waldo really thinking?

Answers on page 122.

The Worst Wizard

I THOUGHT YOU SAID "SECRET WARTS"!

AGE, YOUTH AND ETERNAL LIFE

The Philosopher's Stone

When Prentiss asked if Wizards live forever, Waldo told him the story of the Alchemists.

BECAUSE THIS SPECIAL GOLD WAS SUPPOSED TO MAKE YOU IMMORTAL, MANY KINGS HIRED ALCHEMISTS TO MAKE IT FOR THEM.

UNFORTUNATELY, NOBODY SUCCEEDED, WHICH MADE THE KINGS VERY ANGRY, AND OFTEN SHORTENED THE ALCHEMISTS' LIVES.

MAYBE I WON'T BE AN ALCHEMIST AFTER ALL.

PITY.

Eternal Life

What do vampires, ghosts and zombies have in common? They all live forever! But would eternal life be good or bad for you?

ETERNAL LIFE IS . . .

GOOD: You get shed-loads of birthday presents.

BAD: You can't find a cake big enough for all the candles.

ETERNAL LIFE IS . . .

GOOD: Your trainers come back into fashion.

BAD: Your trainers go out of fashion.

ETERNAL LIFE IS . . .

GOOD: You can try every flavour of ice cream ever invented.

BAD: You only get one set of permanent teeth.

ETERNAL LIFE IS . . .

GOOD: You make masses of friends.

BAD: They're too old to play with.

Age 50 Years in 5 Minutes

Prentiss wanted to look older so Waldo cast an Ageing Spell upon him. Trouble is, Prentiss looked as old and wrinkly as Grewsum the Witch!

CRACK AN EGG
THAT'S RAW AND WHOLE
PUT THE
CONTENTS IN A
BOWL...

EGG
BOWL

KEEP THE YOLK
BUT LOSE THE
WHITE
(USE AN EGG-CUP,
HOLD IT TIGHT!)

EGG
WOBL

MIX THE YOLK WITH ALL YOUR POWER
ADD A PINCH OF SNOW-WHITE FLOUR...

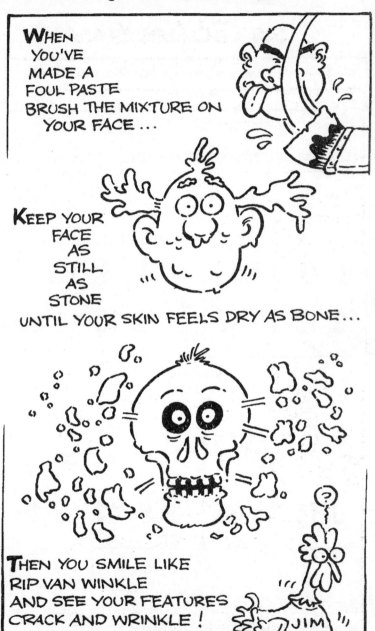

WHEN
 YOU'VE
 MADE A
 FOUL PASTE
 BRUSH THE MIXTURE ON
  YOUR FACE ...

KEEP YOUR
 FACE
 AS
 STILL
 AS
 STONE
UNTIL YOUR SKIN FEELS DRY AS BONE...

THEN YOU SMILE LIKE
RIP VAN WINKLE
AND SEE YOUR FEATURES
CRACK AND WRINKLE !

JIM

Age, Youth and Eternal Life

How Old Are You?

Wizard Waldo can work out your age with these magic cards!
Make your own and impress your friends!

Cut out four cards and copy one of these number groups on to each card:

8	9	10	11
12	13	14	15

4	5	6	7
12	13	14	15

2	3	6	7
10	11	14	15

1	3	5	7
9	11	13	15

Fair or Foul?

Look at the portrait below. Nat-the-Rat sees a pretty young woman with a diamond choker. Hairball sees an old crone like Grewsum. Who is right?

WHAT A BABE!

RATS ARE WEIRD...

80

Answer on page 122.

Lead Into Gold

Witch Grewsum is trying to turn lead into gold. She can only change one letter at a time. Which two words should she put into the spaces?

L E A D

_ _ _ _

_ _ _ _

G O L D

SOON I SHALL BE RICH!

Answer on page 122.

81

The Worst Wizard

NOW YOU SEE IT ...!

The Magic Scroll

Waldo took Prentiss into a dungeon full of ancient scrolls and unrolled one covered in mysterious symbols . . .

Answer on page 122.

Happy and Sad

Can you draw a face that looks happy and sad at the same time? Waldo shows you how!

Copy or trace Waldo's face below on to a piece of paper. Cut round it along the straight lines.
Be real careful with those scissors!

1

2

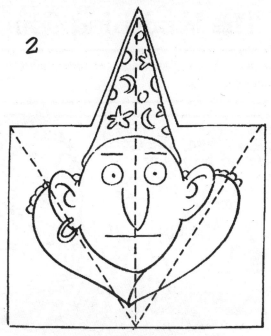

Fold the paper face carefully along the dotted lines.

All you have to do now is to tilt it UP – and it looks sad, and DOWN and it looks happy! Clever, eh?

3

The Vanishing Coin

As Prentiss watched, Waldo made a coin vanish before his very eyes! You can try it too . . .

Fish Wish!

Grewsum challenged Waldo to do real magic, so Waldo turned a peasant into a fish!

CUT THESE LETTERS OUT OF BLACK PAPER.

PEASANT

CUT PIECES OFF EACH LETTER AS SHOWN, UNTIL YOU'RE LEFT WITH THE LETTERS F-I-S-H.

GLUE THE LETTERS F-I-S-H ON TO A PIECE OF WHITE CARD. CAREFULLY ADD THE UNGLUED PIECES SO IT READS P-E-A-S-A-N-T AGAIN.

PEASANT

READ THE SPELL IN A DRAMATIC VOICE, AND ON THE WORD "WISH!" BLOW ALL THE UNGLUED BITS OF PAPER AWAY.

Let the Duck See the Rabbit!

Prentiss didn't understand the spell, so he couldn't turn the Duck into a Rabbit. Can you?

TO WOULD-BE-WIZARDS EVERYWHERE,
HOLD THESE PAGES IF YOU DARE!

AND IF YOU WANT THE RABBIT FOUND,
LIFT THE BOOK AND TURN IT ROUND!

The Worst Wizard

A Grimoire* of Wizard Jokes

Which wizard invention lets
you see through walls?
Windows!

What flies on a stick but doesn't
get anywhere?
A flag!

What's a Wizard's favourite food?
A box of Twix.

What do you call a Wizard
with a golf club on his head?
Harry Putter!

How do we know Robin Hood was a Wizard?
He stole from the witch and gave to the poor!

* Grimoire = a medieval spell book.

THE WEATHER

Clouds Can Talk!

As Waldo told Prentiss, one way to tell the future is to ask the clouds . . .

The Weather

Fluffy and white?
Sunny and Bright!

Flat, thick and grey?
What a Wet Day!

Piled up in towers?
Stormy for hours!

Wisps of White Hair?
Settled and Fair.

The Weather

Make Me A Rainbow

As it was a sunny day, Wizard Waldo decided to show Prentiss how to make a Rainbow. You can try it too!

Put a shallow bowl near the window and fill it with water.

Put a mirror half under the water, facing the sun.

Prop a large piece of white card up beside the bowl.

Move the mirror until the sun reflects off the underwater mirror on to the paper.

Grewsum's Spell for Making Rain

When Prentiss tried Grewsum's Rainmaking Spell, Waldo made him scrub floors for a month!

Open every jar and bottle,
Milk and cola, squash and pickle,
Run upstairs and tip them over,
Through the floorboards let them trickle.

Look behind the fridge and freezer,
Find their switches, shut them down.
Leave their doors ajar for ages
Till the ice has melted down.

The Weather

Turn the taps on bath and basins,
Hide the plugs where no one goes.
Block the loo with wads of paper,
Flush until it overflows.

Activate the neighbours' sprinklers,
Pump the pool out, block the drains,
Stick the hosepipe through the window,
Keep on going till . . . it rains!

Tornado Time

The next day it was raining so the Wizard and his pupil stayed inside. But Prentiss still had a chance to make a tornado!

IT'S RAINING CATS AND DOGS!

REALLY?

THAT'S IMPOSSIBLE!

ACTUALLY IT SOMETIMES RAINS FISH OR EVEN FROGS!

A TORNADO CAN WHIP CREATURES UP FROM A LAKE INTO THE CLOUDS AND THEN 'RAIN' THEM DOWN SOMEWHERE ELSE!

CAN I MAKE A TORNADO?

UH-OH

PUT SOME FIZZY WATER IN A BEAKER.

NOW STIR IT AS FAST AS YOU CAN.

JUST ADD A TEASPOON OF SALT.. AND THERE'S YOUR TORNADO!

COOL!

YOU CAN ALSO ADD FOOD COLOURING OR INK FOR A BETTER EFFECT!

DON'T ENCOURAGE HIM.

Grewsum's Spell for Instant Snow

The Worst Wizard

How to Make a Wand

This easy-to-make wand will complete your new Wizard look!

You need:
- piece of strong paper
- colour pens
- pencil
- paper glue
- tinsel

Draw a line on the piece of paper, 2 cm from the right-hand edge.

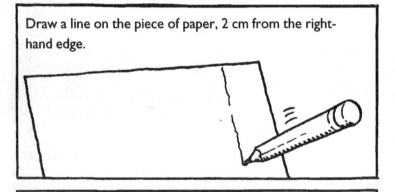

Decorate this strip with one of these cool designs.

Put a line of glue on the back of the decorated strip.

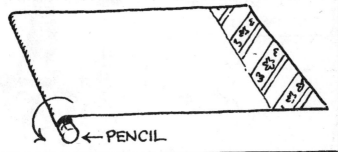

Starting at the unglued end, roll the paper tightly around a pencil and hold it until the glue has set.

← PENCIL

Remove the pencil, stuff the tinsel in both ends of the tube and your Wand is ready!

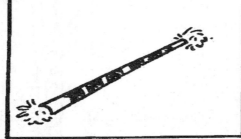

A Broomful of Wizard Jokes

What do you call a witch with
potatoes in her ears?
Anything you like, she can't hear you!

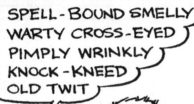

SPELL-BOUND SMELLY
WARTY CROSS-EYED
PIMPLY WRINKLY
KNOCK-KNEED
OLD TWIT

What is a wizard's favourite TV show?
Stars in your Eyes!

When is it bad luck to be
followed by a black cat?
When you're a mouse!

What is a witch's favourite
TV show?
Changing Brooms!

What do you call a Wizard who has
been buried underground for 80 years?
Pete!

TIME AND SPACE

Altering Time

Wizards are strictly forbidden to alter time in case they alter history and erase themselves! But there are lots of safe ways to change your own time . . .

TO SLOW DOWN TIME . . .
Go to Venus, where one day lasts 243 Earth days!

TO SPEED UP TIME . . .
Go to New York on a supersonic jet and get there before you left!

TO REVERSE TIME . . .

Go to Kiribati, an island in the Pacific Ocean – time there is two hours behind everyone else!

TO STOP TIME . . .

Go round the earth at the speed of light!

Birth Day Calculator

Do you know what DAY of the week you were born? Ask your folks, then use Grewsum's handy verse to work out what kind of kid you really are!

Monday's Child is a Disgrace,
Tuesday's Child looks like a Plaice,
Wednesday's Child is very slow,
Thursday's Child chews her toe,
Friday's Child is lazy and greedy,
Saturday's Child is dozy and weedy,
But Sunday's Child is worst of all –
Ugly and mean,
just like
Hairball!

Reversing Time

Prentiss should have got up just after 5.00 a.m. — but he overslept! Waldo's spell put the clock back. How did he do it, and what time is it NOW?

IF YOU'RE ASLEEP LIKE THE DEAD
AND YOU REALLY CAN'T GET OUT OF BED
LET YOUR HAND SLIDE
TO THE CLOCK BY YOUR SIDE
AND TRY TURNING TIME ON ITS HEAD!

Now turn the book upside down!

Answer on page 122.

The 13-Hour Clock

Waldo took Prentiss to the Clock Room to show him the magical
13-Hour Clock

Time Machine

When *Grewsum's Time Machine* went wrong, Prentiss was asked to rewire it. Can you help him match the pictures to the times?

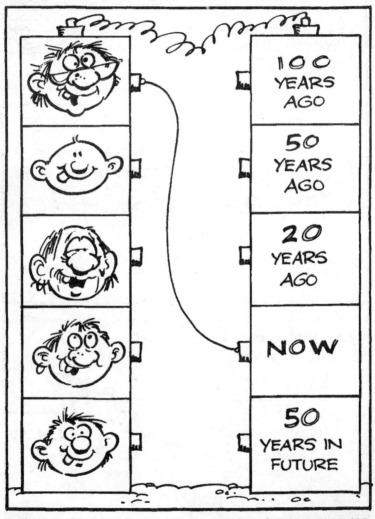

Answers on page 122.

Ode to Time

It's about time Hairball produced one of his poems . . . about Time!

I have cat, just cat.
Cat wasted, a precious cat.
Minute cat of my cat.
Life, cat!
Reading this cat.
Out.

Now *you* say it missing out the word "cat".

Time to Fly

Prentiss wondered what it felt like to fly on a magic broom. So Waldo found a way to show him . . . and you!

Put an ordinary household broom between two chairs.

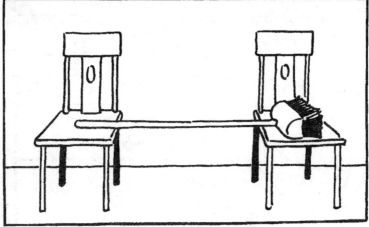

Climb aboard, and put your feet on a cushion.

Ask a friend to push down with their hands on your shoulders for 15 seconds.

Quickly close your eyes as your friend lifts the front of the broom up about 5 cm . . . You're flying!

Grewsum's
Words of Wizzdom

If at first you don't succeed . . .

CHEAT!

ANSWERS

Page 16: Clear the Room Spell
Badgers Smell, Grandma's Warts, Old Dog's Spittle, Plug Hole
Hair, Cheesy Toes

Page 18: Magic Door
Abracadabra

Page 27: Stripe it Lucky
I'm a Zebra (in the stripes on his neck).

Page 28: Talking Turkey
What's the BUZZ?
Frog's got a new sCOOter.
He's been ROARing around on it.
His GOBBLE be his downfall.
There goes the NEIGHbourhood.
HOW Lucky can you get.
Hey Cow! Fancy a dRIVE To the seaside.
I'd rather jump over the MOOn.

Page 34: Beastly Spell
If my cider you have drunk,
You will grow an elephant's TRUNK
Comb of CHICKEN, Wings of BAT
TONGUE of viper, Teeth of CAT
Tail of SQUIRREL, Stripes of BEE
FROG legs just below the knee . . .

Page 42: Grewsum's Vanishing Spell
Candle, Egg, Glass, Prentiss' fork, Prentiss' knife, Pepper pot,
Waldo's hat, Waldo's fork.

Answers

Page 46: Night Creature
An Owl

Pages 54, 55: Test Your Powers
A – 1, B – 2, C – 2, D – 3

Page 56: Crystal Ball
You will be visited by a tall dark stranger wearing a big black hat.

Page 69: Scrambled Egghead
SPUD IT = STUPID
BUG HARMER = HAMBURGER
DEBRA = BEARD
CLOUD RAN = CAULDRON
TEN FOUR = FORTUNE

Page 80: Fair or Foul
Both – it's an optical illusion.

Page 81: Lead into Gold
LEAD, LOAD, GOAD, GOLD

Page 85: Magic Scroll
Upside down and in a mirror it reads CRYSTAL.

Page 113: Reversing Time
If you turn the page upside down, the clock reads:
NOW 05.11.

Page 116: Time Machine
1 – D, 2 – A, 3 – E, 4 – C, 5 – B